After Adolescence

Andi Jackson

Presentation by *BookLeaf Publishing*

Web: www.bookleafpub.com

E-mail: info@bookleafpub.com

ISBN: 9789357444163

First edition 2022

DEDICATION

To my other half and our beasties.

ACKNOWLEDGEMENT

I want to acknowledge my co. Without her, I would never have had the courage to do this.

PREFACE

When I first started this collection, I was navigating through my final year of college. I was finishing up my minor in creative writing and my inspiration was found in every little experience, muddy paw, sticky hands, happy grins and warm hugs. This is my journey through my years, pre-thirty.

Falling

It all happened so fast

You took my heart in a storm

a storm of love and passion

It happened before I knew it

I fell so fast

I couldn't catch myself

Now I lie here broken

Waiting for you

To give me a hand

Back on my feet

And back in your arms

And there I will find,

that you will always be mine.

Hazel

Today your eyes are grey
Waves, -kushhh-, are cresting
Ships slowly sway
You. Never resting.

Today your eyes are green
Lazily dreaming
No troubles to be seen
Slow drum beat-ba-beating

Today your eyes are blue
Heavy heart
Needing something to do
Sadness tearing you apart.

Hazel Eyes,
Since I met you
Feelings you cannot disguise
Color always ringing true
Never telling lies
Grey, green or blue
My Husband's, Hazel Eyes.

Dear Baby Love,

Hello.
Your mother here.
We haven't met yet.
I hope we do,
If we don't, I need you to know.

I love you more than the water in the sea
I wanted you more than anything
Grow big and strong like a tree
Go see things and learn and just be

When night falls and you wonder,
"What would she think of me?"
I think you are bold, brave and daring.
I think you are scared, happy and wondering

I dream of the day you share a love with me
The day you have a baby of your own
I dream of you scraping your knee
Crying "Mommy, help me"

You have your father to guide you
And my spirit will always follow you
No matter the distance
You are always in my heart.

I'm sorry my body failed you
I'm sorry I can't see you graduate
I am so very proud of you
I hope you never hesitate

Just so I know you know,
I love you so.

Growing Love

There it is.
Hands are trembling
Heart is racing.
Sweat breaks out on my brow.
I set it down.
I'll do laundry.

There she is.
Today she is wearing colorful scrubs of pink and
purple.
She hands me a slip of paper.
11.27.2015
It's confirmed but it's as if I'm a clean slate.
Blank.

Ooooh...I'm stuck on a ceaseless merry go round
Round and round.
No relief in sight.
Sleep washes over me in waves
Barely coherent.

There we are.
Swelling past my toes.
My eyes finally open.
My heart is heavy and reality crashes in.

A galloping heartbeat rings in my ears.

There you are.
A little flutter from within.
My heart swells as we share a moment.
All ours, and I pray I make it through delivery
day.

Today is delivery day.
Rushing,
excitement,
nervousness,
Fear.

You cry and I unwind like a curl pulled loose.
Then springing back into place, as they whisk
you away.
I'm bleeding... and you're barely breathing.

We made it.
Again we connect.
Your tiny body pressed against mine.
My little Roo, I your Kanga.
I try to nourish you, you're too weak right now,
We'll try again later.

As we sit.

The creaking of the chair comforts you as you
doze off.
The sun filters in the side of the curtain,
Illuminating your soft features.
You grip my finger so tight I feel it all the way
to my heart.
A wave of sunlight and radiance wash over me.
Rocking comforts me as my heart swells to
aching.
The soft rise and fall signals sleep.
I squeeze you closer,
lavender and chamomile creep into my nose and
I cherish you.
My healthy,
happy boy.
My love.

My New ABC's

Absolutely adoring a
Beautiful baby boy
Carefully crashing,
Deliberately destroying,
Effortlessly
Flourishing.

Gaily gallivanting grelim,
Harping
Illogically.
Joyously joking.
Knowing kindness,
Loving
Mommy.

Nearly nodding naps,
Obliviously,
Persistently,
Quietly
Resting.
Sleepy slumbers.

Taking tumbles
Under

Various
Weathered
X-cursions.
Youthful
Zeal.

Mommy, Why?

Laughter twinkles through the baby monitor.
No alarms this morning.
Wake up.
Get baby.
Make breakfast.

No! Don't touch that!
Why?
Because, baby love, it's hot.

Eggs are done.
Hangry baby screaming
eggs hidden in the freezer.

You can't have them yet.
Why?
Because they will burn your mouth.

Baby into high chair.
Recover eggs from freezer.

Sit down!
Why?
Because you will fall and get hurt!

Breakfast is over.
Change a diaper.

No!
Keep your hands back.
Why?
Because it's icky and can make you sick!

Run off and play.
Mommy pick up the house.

Toys here.
Toys there.
Toys back in the toy box.

No!
Don't put that in your mouth!
Why?
Because you could choke.

Watch a movie.
The Mommy is tired.
Nap time soon.

No!
Don't jump on the couch!
Why?
Because you will get hurt.

Do dishes.
Pick toys back up.
Read Brown Bear Brown Bear.
Read it again.
And once more.
Chase baby through the house.
Remote in the bath tub.
Phone is in the laundry basket.
Baby's lovey in the trash.
Rescue everything from the baby.
Make lunch.
Repeat.
Make dinner.
Repeat.
Have a bath.
Read a book.
Time for bed.

Why?
Because I said so.

Moon Dance

I see you
Peeking through my window
Stars dance with you
And yet you still whisper
Come to me
Dance with me child
Drink me up and be free

The air is crisp
My breath floats up to greet you
Your light blesses my skin
And I do not burn
My feet float upon the earth
Damp with dew
As I dance with you

Intrusive

He has the face of an angel
Perfect smile, perfect nose
His eyes full of love, life, and wonder
                                           I can't

do this any longer

She flutters from within
The flips, the flops
Her presence unmistakable as she grows
                                I don't want to

wake up tomorrow.

He rubs my feet, paints my toes
Kind eyes, warm hugs
His endless love and affection always show
                                   I give up,

please just let me go.

The pain,
 the stress,
 the hormones
        Course through my body
            Slice through my mind

Break up my peace
Push me to leave
Force me to...

Just disappear.

Banshee

Ten tiny fingers
Ten tiny toes
Clawed tips
Snarled nose

The banshee sings her song tonight
The outside moon is shinning bright
Shriekers, she wails
Her song cannot be quailed

Then night turns to day
And Squeakers is here to stay
Coos and squeaks
My dear monster sleeps

Smokey April Days

Smoke
Breathes into the wind

Sun
Dances on my skin

Birds chirp,
Squirrels chatter

A song,
A melody weaving through the air

My toes
Kissed by this mornings dew

My heels dig into the soft soil
My toe rejoice in the coolness of the earth

A breeze
Shuffling through the trees

Red buds, white flowers
Drifting to the ground

A cat

Dressed in a tuxedo
Chased by toddling toes
Dances between the trees.

A scene,
A dream,
A memory
Of a life that is a Smokey April Day

Sour Patch Day

Today is a sour patch day.
First it's sour
Then it's sweet

Perpetually sixteen
Can't miss a beat

No time to remain dower
Today is a treat

Our sweet
Today she is one

A gift from you
A bandage I'm sure

Today we feast
Hearts ache but endure

Carrot cake for you
Presents for her.

When Spring Comes

Green grass, pale blue sky
Yellow slide, goes round and round
Bright squeals, down down down.

It's

It's pancakes in the morning
Meltdowns over Mom's coffee

It's park runs and sandy britches
"Stop hitting your brother" and "Love your
sister"

It's shrieking hour and hangry babes
Lunch on the floor, snacks for the dogs

It's matching pjs and goofy games
Roughhousing with dad and tickling mom

It's Sunday morning bacon
None left for dad.

It's showers and baths,
Streaking through the house.

It's the ups, downs, and sideways
Messy days full of love.

It's bad days and sibling rivalry
"GO TO YOU ROOM!", " Leave that alone!"

It's "Get out of the kitchen", and "Feed the
dogs"
Helping mom make noodles

All these things and more,
In this messy, messy world.
What more could I ask for?
My perfectly imperfect life unfurled.

Who Am I?

A baby, fresh and new
a name for just me and you

I am my father's daughter
My brother's sister

I am my husband's wife
My son's mother

These relationships
Birth me anew

A New Promise:
VII.XX.MMXX

For ten years
we have done battle.
Some days
against each other,
some days
alongside one another

      despite our struggles
         It was all together.

Two babies,
they have shown us
how much love
we were capable of,
how much fear
we could feel
and the amazing
blinding
rage

      that I have only felt
        in parenthood.

We have felt deep
fathomless
pain
From grief
from losing pets
From losing family

     From watching friends
       Come and go

Navigating life's events:
Holidays and
birthdays,
picnics and
barbecues.
Weddings and
baby showers,
work parties and
house warmings

     where my plus one
       is always you.

I made promises the first time.
Some I kept,
Some I fell short.
This time,
I think,

I know better what to say.
I remember writing my vows then
all I could think was
"I love him, that much I know."

      now I know
            how to show it as well.

I promise to
Consider your feelings
to love you
in your language.
To build you up
to compliment you more.

I promise to
swallow my pride
To not be a
petulant beast
when you call me out.
To be your number one fan.

I promise to
remind you
we all have shortcomings
but
with each place we fall short,
We excel in extraordinary ways.

I've loved you this long,
I'll love you much longer,

    For now
        For eternity
            I'll love you.

Act I: The Last First Day

Bright eyed and bushy tailed.
Check and check,
Each and every detail.
Nerves! Then sweat beads on my neck

It's the last first day.
A mountain of tasks
Paving the way to May-
I sure hope I can last!

Excitement charges the air
An empty classroom,
But all my students are there.
"Cameras on!", I scan the digital room.

Hello, I am Mrs. Hot Face and clammy palms.
Silence welcomes me, anxiety consumes me.
Ms. Mentor is there, she takes the coms.
A storm rages, but she releases me.

Act II: Testing, Testing, 1-2

Confidence is growing,
Missteps at every turn.
Encouraging words bubble to overflowing,
Next mistake is a chance to learn.

Compliments and praises
Feedback and critique
Drive for success, constantly raises-
Another bump to hone my technique

Lesson plan when I eat
Lesson plan when I sleep
Never stopping to miss a beat
Exhaustion sets in while I weep.

It is time, the big event
The teacher's portfolio-
biggest project to present-
Now to let my knowledge flow

Act III: Desolate Defeat

It's opening day
I take the stage-
It is time to act out this play.
Little did I know of the war to wage.

Up in flames-
Confidence shattered
The student, she claims
"The President's name is being battered!"

One small step,
One giant mess,
New promises made to be kept-
Now to sort out the rest.

Drowning in tears of frustration
Gasping through the oceans of despair
Surging through trials and tribulation
Finding my truth to ensnare.

Act IV: At The Close

Looking back from where I started
A million miles away from today
I see the growth and how I departed
From ideal to real somehow, someway.

Bright eyed and bushy tailed.
My heart so full, it feels maimed
"I will stay strong," but to no avail
Teary eyes barely contained.

My kids of eighteen
Preparing for graduation
Together, I found us at an in between
Making our ways in a new direction.

Mere months feel like forever,
Fleeting moments,
A mountainous endeavor,
Lasting relationships made only once.

Things My 8th Graders Say

"Class, please get your book"
Bruh, why you do me like that?
When's class out again?
Can I go to the bathroom?
Huh? Wait, what are we doing?

Dreaming In Pen

I'll be a writer,
that's what I said
I'll make it,
a book,
I'll prove it-
You'll see!

That blank page
haunts my dreams
'till a melody fills me
And I am bursting at the seams!

Inspiration
comes from all places;
A stray sun beam
A sniffle
or sneeze
A squeal
A scream
110 degrees.

But look here,
I've clawed through the clutter
And managed to muster
A book,

My poems,
For all to see

I am
So proud
Of me.